P9-CLS-596

I am a
Chameleon

Aaron Carr

LET'S READ
AV2 BY WEIGL
ADDED VALUE • AUDIO VISUAL
www.av2books.com

LET'S READ

AV²

BY WEIGL™

ADDED VALUE · AUDIO VISUAL

Go to **www.av2books.com**, and enter this book's unique code.

BOOK CODE

C382628

AV² by Weigl brings you media enhanced books that support active learning.

AV² provides enriched content that supplements and complements this book. Weigl's AV² books strive to create inspired learning and engage young minds in a total learning experience.

Your AV² Media Enhanced books come alive with...

Audio
Listen to sections of the book read aloud.

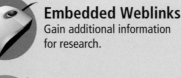

Video
Watch informative video clips.

Embedded Weblinks
Gain additional information for research.

Try This!
Complete activities and hands-on experiments.

Key Words
Study vocabulary, and complete a matching word activity.

Quizzes
Test your knowledge.

Slide Show
View images and captions, and prepare a presentation.

... and much, much more!

Published by AV² by Weigl
350 5th Avenue, 59th Floor   New York, NY   10118
Websites: www.av2books.com   www.weigl.com

Copyright ©2016 AV² by Weigl
All rights reserved. No part of this publication may be reproduced, stored in a retrieval system, or transmitted in any form or by any means, electronic, mechanical, photocopying, recording, or otherwise, without the prior written permission of the publisher.

Library of Congress Cataloging-in-Publication Data

Carr, Aaron.
 Chameleon / Aaron Carr.
    pages cm. -- (I am)
 ISBN 978-1-4896-2625-7 (hardcover : alk. paper) -- ISBN 978-1-4896-2626-4 (softcover : alk. paper) -- ISBN 978-1-4896-2627-1 (single-user ebk.) --
ISBN 978-1-4896-2628-8 (multi-user ebk.)
1. Chameleons--Juvenile literature. I. Title.
 QL666.L23C37 2014
 597.95--dc23
                                    2014038573

Printed in the United States of America in North Mankato, Minnesota
1 2 3 4 5 6 7 8 9 0 18 17 16 15 14

112014
WEP311214

Senior Editor: Heather Kissock   Art Director: Terry Paulhus

Weigl acknowledges Getty Images, iStockphoto, and Corbis as the primary image suppliers for this title.

I am a Chameleon

In this book, I will teach you about

- **myself**
- **my food**
- **my home**
- **my family**

and much more!

3

I am a chameleon.

I can make myself look like a rainbow.

I change colors to show how I feel.

I can look to the
left and right at
the same time.

I have a tongue that is longer than my body.

13

I can catch food in
the blink of an eye.

I can sleep hanging upside down.

17

I wrap my tail around branches to keep from falling.

I need a warm home
with many trees.

I am a chameleon.

CHAMELEON FACTS

These pages provide detailed information that expands on the interesting facts found in the book. They are intended to be used by adults as a learning support to help young readers round out their knowledge of each amazing animal featured in the *I Am* series.

Pages 4–5

I am a chameleon. Chameleons are reptiles. They are a type of lizard. There are more than 150 species of chameleons. Chameleons vary in size between species, ranging in length from 1 inch (2.5 centimeters) to 27 inches (68.6 cm). The name chameleon means "earth lion" in ancient Greek.

Pages 6–7

I can make myself look like a rainbow. A chameleon's skin is made up of several layers. The outer layer is transparent. The other layers each contain pigments that create different colors, including yellow, red, blue, white, and brown. Chameleons can mix these pigments to create an even wider range of colors.

Pages 8–9

I change colors to show how I feel. A chameleon's color often depends on its mood. An excited chameleon may be red, while a calm chameleon might be green. In addition to communication, chameleons also use color to help maintain a comfortable body temperature.

Pages 10–11

I can look to the left and right at the same time. Chameleons can move their eyes independently. This allows them to look in different directions at the same time. They can also rotate their eyes to look in all directions, giving them 360-degree vision. Thick eyelids with a tiny opening for the pupil protect the eyes from damage.

Pages 12–13

I have a tongue that is longer than my body.

I have a tongue that is longer than my body. A chameleon's tongue can be up to twice its body length. The chameleon relies on its tongue to catch the insects it eats. The tip of the tongue forms a pouch as it makes contact with the prey. The pouch works like a suction cup to grab and hold onto the insect.

Pages 14–15

I can catch food in the blink of an eye.

I can catch food in the blink of an eye. A chameleon's tongue is like a catapult that launches toward its prey. The internal structure of bones, tissues, and muscles allows the tongue to travel toward prey at a high speed. Scientists have recorded chameleon tongue strikes accelerating at speeds similar to those of fighter jets.

Pages 16–17

I can sleep hanging upside down.

I can sleep hanging upside down. Most chameleons are tree-dwellers. Their feet help them grip tree branches. The front feet have two outside toes grouped together and three inside toes grouped together. This is reversed in the rear feet. These toes allow chameleons to keep a firm grip on each side of a branch. They can stay attached to the branch even when upside down and sleeping.

Pages 18–19

I wrap my tail around branches to keep from falling. Many chameleon species have prehensile tails. This means they can use their long tails to hold on to objects. When climbing, a chameleon may wrap its tail around branches like a coil. This helps it stay balanced while moving and climbing in trees and bushes.

I wrap my tail around branches to keep from falling.

Pages 20–21

I need a warm home with many trees.

I am a chameleon.

I need a warm home with many trees. Chameleons have adapted to life in forests, deserts, and mountains. They are found in Africa, Asia, the Middle East, and Europe. About half of all chameleon species live in Madagascar. Habitat loss is becoming an issue for chameleons there. Some chameleon species only found in Madagascar are now endangered.

KEY WORDS

Research has shown that as much as 65 percent of all written material published in English is made up of 300 words. These 300 words cannot be taught using pictures or learned by sounding them out. They must be recognized by sight. This book contains 37 common sight words to help young readers improve their reading fluency and comprehension. This book also teaches young readers several important content words, such as proper nouns. These words are paired with pictures to aid in learning and improve understanding.

Page	Sight Words First Appearance	Page	Content Words First Appearance
4	a, am, I	4	chameleon
6	can, like, look, make	6	rainbow
8	change, how, show, to	8	colors
10	and, at, left, right, same, the, time	12	body, tongue
12	have, is, my, than, that	18	branches, tail
14	an, eye, food, in, of		
16	down		
18	around, from, keep		
20	home, many, need, trees, with		

AV2 BY WEIGL™
MEDIA ENHANCED BOOKS
ADDED VALUE • AUDIO VISUAL

Check out av2books.com for activities, videos, audio clips, and more!

1 Go to av2books.com

2 Enter book code C382628

3 Explore your chameleon book!

www.av2books.com